The Ocean of Livingness

The Ocean of Livingness

Opening to Celebrate Cosmic Life

By Don C. Nix, J.D., Ph.D.

iUniverse, Inc.
New York Bloomington

The Ocean of Livingness
Opening to Celebrate Cosmic Life

iUniverse books may be ordered through booksellers or by contacting:

iUniverse
1663 Liberty Drive
Bloomington, IN 47403
www.iuniverse.com
1-800-Authors (1-800-288-4677)

ISBN: 978-1-4502-6972-8 (sc)
ISBN: 978-1-4502-6971-1 (ebook)

Printed in the United States of America

iUniverse rev. date: 11/04/2010

Dedication

To Brian Swimme, whose combination of scientific rigor and wonder fired my imagination, opened my mind and created new vistas in my perceptions of Macro reality. With great appreciation.

Don C. Nix
Sonoma, Ca
October, 2010

Contents

Introduction

The unfolding of the Cosmos is a single, uninterrupted creative event from the Big Bang to us. This new and very recent realization has arisen out of the discovery of Quantum Physics that Reality is not a collection of separate objects floating in space and colliding with each other, but rather a single thing, a single web of complete inter-connection. Actually, even the phrase "web of inter-connection" still carries traces of the separateness that we have projected onto Reality for the last 400 years. The actual vision of Quantum Physics is that the Cosmos is a total singularity. It has no separate aspects that could harbor a localized creativity. If creativity exists anywhere in the Field, then it must exist throughout the Field, because there are no boundaries of localized separation within the Field. And, the Field is the Cosmos in all Its vast and magnificent size. Thus, creativity within the Field is omnipresent and uninterrupted from the beginning to the present moment, and it will continue to be so into the unlimited future. It is simply the nature of the Field. We are the Cosmos in its latest and most articulated configuration.

The additional realization that is blooming now, though science is not yet ready to go there, is that the universe is alive and aware. Consciousness and intelligence are not located only within the human and a few other organisms, but are qualities of the Field, found throughout. Again, there are no localized places within the Field that could harbor separate islands of consciousness and life. If consciousness and life exist anywhere in the Field, then they exist everywhere within it. The completed picture of the new vision of Reality is that we live in a single, vast Field of living consciousness that constantly throws up, materializes and sustains the material realm and then re-absorbs it, constantly evolving new forms. This tracks, to a remarkable and minute degree, the ancient Hindu concept of Brahman. This ancient knowledge, probably 5,000 years old and perhaps much, much older, was formulated not through the analysis, empirical study and rational examination used by our current scientific model, but through direct experience of the Cosmos. The ancients looked carefully at the Reality around them, went inside and used pure intuition to arrive at their insights. This should be a little humbling to our present-day scientists, who are inclined to dismiss all aspects of human knowledge not obtained through their preferred procedures. We are larger, and the Cosmos is larger, than science can unveil with its investigations into matter. We need to harness intuitive insights to our scientific inquiry in order to move forward into a larger, future worldview.

That larger worldview will include the vision that we exist inside an Ocean of Livingness—miraculous, alive, creative, and conscious. If we can grow ourselves into this realization, then we can once again live in a universe of deep and profound meaning. We are yearning and longing for that. The 77 poems in this little book are an attempt to enter this new "Quantum Consciousness." We are living in a time of great transition, when our understanding of Macro-reality is shifting radically. It is an interesting time to be alive on the earth.

1

How is it to be a wave
in a vast and mysterious Sea?
Thrown up from the depths,
taking a form,
metamorphosing,
leaping and arching,
cresting and troughing,
and totally caught
in motion's intensity.
In the midst of all the turbulence,
when you're frothing and foaming
on the surface,
it's easy to forget the Sea.
It's tempting to think
that the power you feel
is coming all from yourself.
It's tempting to yield to the project
of growing yourself ever larger.
It's restless on the surface.
Other waves are all around.
It's tempting to compare and compete and,
to grow yourself,
pull away their water.
In the ceaseless roil and roll of the Sea
in the repetitions of your days,
as you're pulled by the currents
and tossed by the wind,
keep in mind that you're magical froth and foam
on the surface of the Sea,
You're never separate,
a bit of flotsam,
on the surface of moving Infinity.

2

Raise your arms and exult!
Sing into the wind
your fierce song of joy.
Dance your dance
of celebration.
Whirl in place until you fall.
You're alive!
You're walking the earth!
Your heart is beating mightily!
You're conscious!
You're sensing the world,
and growing and changing,
held in a living Sea
of miracle and mystery!
Let it in.
Let it all in.
Lift your eyes.
Raise your arms.
Now.
Let your celebration begin.

3

Before my amazed eyes,
and totally outside my will,
I'm touched by infinite Power,
called to become a shaman,
invoking and leading others
into the invisible realms,
and thrown into fierce
and unrequited joy.
I'm called to do my little part
to lift the weariness,
to raise the heads,
to wake the sleeping minds.
Pushed from above,
and below,
and from every direction around me,
I am electrified into my dance,
spinning and whirling,
and a little disoriented by it all,
I am thrown into violent motion.
There's something burning here.

4

Pluto arrives from the Underworld
to break open a rigid and reified world,
to crack into pieces the temples of priests
of a religion that has outlived its time.
The city gates cannot be preserved.
The gate-keepers now are toppled.
Above and through the piles of stones
the fresh breeze of the future blows.

5

What shall I say?
What shall I convey?
Every thread that I pull
unravels the Whole.
Every drop that I taste
contains the Ocean.
To pick a thread and
pull it free
leaves everything else unsaid.
The Cosmos is a singularity,
a unity from the top of the Sea
to the depths of Its Cosmic ocean-bed.

6

I'm waiting for Your inspiration.
Fire my mind.
Flood my spirit.
Usher me into Your realm of Light,
and electrify my pulsing nerves.
I am an empty husk,
waiting and yearning
for the influx of Your Majesty,
to bring me fully and truly alive.

7

Trapped in my smallness,
I sit.
Mired in my flatness,
I yearn.
Caught in my thoughts,
I reach for the depths
and the vastness of Living Mind.
I know that all around me
Brilliancy sparkles and glints,
but my eyes are too dim
and my soul is too small
to touch this radiant Life.
I think I must learn to reach deeper
with my heart and with my cells.
I must learn how,
without map or guide,
to pierce these earthly veils.

8

I watch as the Cosmos unfolds Itself,
emerging from nothing to something,
efflorescing Its way to material form,
with meaning at Its heart.
I hold my breath in astonishment,
to see the vast complexity,
and the fierce intelligence,
and the stunning beauty,
that the Cosmos throws up all around me.

9

Life is rising to the surface.
It will burst into reality.
The future is already here,
held in potentiality.
The people of the future
are waiting now to be,
restless,
impatient to have their turn,
to emerge from
the vast and roiling Sea.
The future is already here.
The past is still with us too.
Time and space are just mental ideas
that belong to an out-dated, dying view.

10

There's so much here we cannot see,
no matter how we try.
Our animal eyes are limited.
We can only see physicality,
the surface of reality.
The beauty,
the meaning,
are all within.
We must feel them with our heart.
We must pierce the veils
of the physical world.
Let's do it now.
Let's make a start.

11

Just in time
the key appeared,
that unlocked the door,
that loosed the torrent,
that covered the world,
that swept it clean,
that opened its heart
and expanded its dreams,
and miraculously gave a new start.

12

Have you ever been thrown away,
jerked from a dream of togetherness
and brutally sent into the night?
Did you take from this
that your value was nil,
that you weren't worth keeping around?
Did you take it as a given that
they were right to throw you away,
like used Kleenex,
or peach pits devoid of fruit?
Why did you arrive at that?
How did you forget
that you are miracle happening,
space incarnated to think and speak,
and walk the Cosmos
and change the world.
You cannot be diminished
by a thoughtless, heedless act.
Your value has its source
in the invisible, boundless Sea
that has selected you
and put you here to sing your song
for just this instant in time.

13

In shaping and crafting the poem
the thunder of stars is distantly heard,
the Infinite comes,
the Real is unleashed,
the bounds of the mind drop away.
The ghosts of things yet unseen
appear in the shadows of thought.
A glimpse is offered
of shimmering realms,
without limits,
without materiality.
Locked in the grip of Potential,
the future is waiting to be.
It begins on this morning of fog,
as the sun comes over the hill to me.

14

My mind is a flow.
My mind is a river,
now inside its banks,
now breaking its bounds.
I cannot tell where
it may go next.
It's not under my control.
I am moved by forces
I cannot see.
I am part of a greater Web.
In struggling to see
what is me and not me,
I am thrown up and moved
by the boundless Sea.

15

Is it for this I came,
to think my thoughts
and fear my fears,
and take part in the human game?
Is this all there is?
I had dreamed of something
magnificent,
and deep,
and profound,
and sacred,
and meaningful.
But I find myself stalled
in my little life.
Each day unfolds like the other.
I must be evolving here.
I must be expanding myself.
But I yearn for the Sea
of Sublimity
to fashion me and use me,
and to push me up, out and further.

16

You cannot fall out of the Ocean of Life.
You can only change your form.
Nothing is ever lost as
we move from one realm to another.
There is no emptiness here.
There is no reason for fear.
We are thrown up temporarily
to experience the domain of matter,
then we're pulled back into the magic Sea,
the vast Sea of Sublimity.
There is nothing here but
Life,
Life,
Life,
all the way down to the bottom.

17

We are each a field,
a unique and personal force,
a center of power and energy,
spilling ourselves into the air
and pouring ourselves into life.
We swim in the Sea
of the Greater Field
that occupies the Cosmos,
invisible,
swirling,
manifesting,
unfolding,
brimming with potential
and throwing up our shimmering world.

18

The inner critic is silenced.
Finally.
After decades of defending myself,
surviving attack after vicious attack,
I have finally shut him up.
I have finally shut him up.
Where his voice was now is silence.
This is a major victory.
I got here not by achievement,
or recognition,
or status,
but rather by overwhelming him
with the miracle that is me,
a primate descended from the apes,
fashioned through eons of time,
endowed with miraculous consciousness,
now raising my eyes to the stars.

19

We are bigger than we suppose.
As we buy our shoes
and cook our food,
and pay our bills
and fear our fears,
we feel that we are tiny.
Trapped in a box of narrowness,
we assume that this is all that's here.
We couldn't be more wrong.
Beyond the thin veil that covers us,
just over the hill of our mind,
an astonishing Force is exploding
our lovely world into being.
A vast Presence is in our world.
Its all around us now.
If we can open the cells of our body
it is there for us to feel.
We can wake ourselves
and blow through our edges
and finally touch the Real.

20

Beauty is in the way the world
is composed with perfect order.
Each thing fits in,
perfectly collated
with every other thing.
The rain hits the prairie.
The flowers wake up
and bloom their way into being.
Life blooms Itself in a similar way.
The world is emerging and pulsing itself
into an unknown, sublime new day.

21

The Cosmos is moving
from dark to light,
one particle at a time.
Black radiance yields
to the luminous glow
of a billion exploding suns.
Our soul is moving
from dark to light,
matching the process,
tracing the unfolding,
finding its future,
deepening its Cosmic Life.

22

Stop your doing
for just a moment
and try to just
let yourself be.
Feel the mysterious life
that is coursing through your veins.
See the miraculous consciousness
that is allowing you to see.
Open your cells.
Open your body.
In a moment of stillness,
break free.

23

How could we have gone so wrong?
What led us so astray?
In the midst of burgeoning miracles
we completely lost our way.
How could we be so self-absorbed
and so lost in our petty greed
that we close our eyes to our fellows
who are in such desperate need?
How can we come together
to create something new and fine?
How can we evolve ourselves
to open our eyes,
and open our hearts,
and live our way
into a day
as a tool for the Divine?

24

The Cosmos is waiting now
for us to lift our heads,
begin our dance,
and sing our songs
in rapturous celebration.
We've been too young to realize
what life is all about.
We see now the terrible costs
of living separately.
We're evolving into the ability
to turn and see infinity,
to see the Whole as a unity,
a blooming singularity.

25

Take these veils from my eyes
and set me free.
Pour your richness into my soul.
Move me deeper into Mystery
Touch my little mind.
Open me to Your miracle.
I feel You with my heart.
I am waiting,
and hoping,
patiently,
for the deepening to start.

26

Singing hymns of praise
is an ancient thing to do.
The bipeds through millennia
have felt the need to do it,
pushed by Something
so magnificent
and incapable of being understood
that the only course
was to begin to dance,
to deepen the trance,
and start to sing in praise.
I am doing it right now.

27

This is my spot on earth.
This is my destiny,
surrounded by my fellows
who are marching now with me
through a human life,
with human fears,
and a burgeoning push to be.
We are all just transient here,
just passing through
to get the view
of Life in the form of matter.
Soon we will leave the earth.
We will have had our marvelous time.
A new set of folks will appear.
Their lives will unfold the future,
profound, chaotic, sublime.

28

Presence all around me.
I feel it with my cells.
I yearn to touch Its livingness.
I want It to envelop my heart.
I want to absorb Its grandeur,
and be soaked in
Its sacredness,
Its depth,
Its beauty,
Its meaning.
I want to be expanded into
the vastness of Cosmic Life.

29

We are on the spinning Earth
that is circling the radiant Sun.
We are in the midst of dance.
If we could let ourselves,
we could raise our arms
and whirl in place,
and enter the spinning reel.
But I think it is not to be.
We are too numb,
and too rigid,
and too unimaginative,
and too locked in place,
to move our joy
into the Livingness
of our surrounding space.

30

Each day comes like a miracle,
full of freshness and potential.
We are given the gift
of a brand new start.
We are given the gift
of a beating heart.
We are privileged to walk the earth.
Take time to feel the gratitude
that your heart must surely feel.
It's a great thing
to be born a human.
Grace is pouring upon you now.
It is pouring upon you this moment,
and every moment that you are here.
Wake up and stir yourself.
Turn toward the Cosmos,
and feel Its pulsing, living heart.

31

There is no darkness
that the Light cannot swallow.
There is goodness
at the heart of Life.
There is meaning emerging here,
out of pain and suffering and strife.
Perhaps we cannot see it.
Our heads are down.
Our eyes are closed.
We cannot perceive the Light.
The Cosmos is unfolding Itself
in Its infinite way
into a new day
that is full of radiance
far beyond our sight.

32

Honor the ones who are dear to you.
They are only here for a minute,
thrown up from the depths of bubbling Life
to walk the earth,
and smile their smiles,
and open their hearts
as you pass nearby.
We need each other's affection
and contact,
and merger,
and good wishes,
to bring ourselves fully to life.

33

Part of me lives in the Realm of Light.
Part of me lives here on Earth.
I seem to be two,
each completely unique,
and very different the one from the other.
One of me pays the insurance.
The other regards the stars.
One of me is locked in separateness.
The other becomes the sky.
We are marching through life,
the two of us,
companions until we die.

34

I have a task
while I'm on this earth
but it's not very clear to me.
I think that I must discover it
in a larger and richer reality.
I must move my mind
to a bigger place.
I must expand myself
into a larger space.
I must open myself
in order to see
why I'm here
and what I must be.

35

There is beauty blooming all around
but we,
lost in our crises and little ambitions,
can't be bothered
to raise our heads and see it.
What a waste of good beauty.
What a waste of good human sensibility.

36

I wake in the early morning,
preoccupied with myself,
and dark in my little world.
I rise.
I watch the sun come up,
and I am filled
with the effulgence
and the ineffable loveliness
of warm Life spreading Itself
across the waking Earth.
My darkness vanishes
into the spilling Living Light.

37

I realize, with some horror,
that I'm unsteady on my feet.
Erosion is taking its toll.
All those decades that
I took for granted
a robust and healthy body,
and a good and clear mind,
and a bright and beckoning future,
are coming due for payment now.
I could have been more aware,
I could have seen more clearly,
I could have realized,
minute by passing minute,
that what the Cosmos bestows on us
must someday be given back.

38

In the early, early morning
I yearn for—
a cup of fragrant coffee,
a warm and crackling fire,
and the silence of a sleeping world.
I could raise my eyes
and yearn for more—
a vision of galaxies foaming,
coalescing and colliding,
exploding, bursting stars
sending their light and life out
into the Living Black,
and lovely, verdant, life-filled worlds,
sailing majestically around their suns,
just as my Earth is doing now.

39

The fire crackles and flares.
My heart beats in time.
The world turns on its axis.
My mind slips its confine.
The Cosmos opens Its door.
The vastness floods my heart.
From the black well of my futility
I sense a brand new start.

40

When I am far from Being
I see through eyes of ice.
The beauty of Earth is hidden.
I am lost in separateness.
In these moments I feel mortality.
The Darkness looms.
The Abyss opens up.
In fear and hesitation,
I reach for the Hand of Life.

41

It's not easy to be human,
to live with frailty every day,
to stumble along without knowing
the reasons or the way.
We live our lives in spite of fear.
Vulnerability is always near.
We search for the reason
that we are here,
but the Universe is silent.

42

Have you ever felt creativity
run coursing through your veins,
its excitement charging your cells,
its energy firing your mind?
Did you think for a moment
that it came from you?
Did you feel like you produced it?
Get over it.
Open your eyes.
That burst of light that your body felt
was coming from the Field of Life,
that produces Spring,
and unfolds the world,
and creates all the new-borns.
We are swimming in It as we speak,
now and forevermore.

43

Futility raises its ugly head.
I beat it back.
It comes again.
I know,
in this moment of blackness,
that the Cosmos has a plan.
It cannot be random or meaningless.
It's far too intricate,
and collated,
and lovely,
and intelligent,
to have been fashioned by
the chaos of chance.
If I cannot see
my place in the plan,
the problem is with my eyes.

44

Busyness does not yield meaning.
To whirl in life so fast
that you cannot,
or will not,
think about the questions
of why you are here,
or why the fiery galaxies
are shining in the sky,
or why the earth is dancing its way
around a radiant sun today
will leave you, in time,
if you don't change your path,
empty, disconnected and desperate.

45

Are You there?
Are You there,
with your powerful electricity
and barely-glimpsed Majesty?
I'm in my chair and reaching.
I'm reaching with my heart.
Will You deign right now to share Yourself
and give me a fresh, new start?

46

My cluttered mind clears for a moment,
as I reach for the silence within.
All around me Presence pulsates,
and I am wafted out of myself.
In this moment I am complete,
and I can clearly see
that my smallness,
my separateness,
my vulnerability,
have vanished into the Cosmic Sea.

47

I go from my perch in my chair in the dawn
to unlimited space above.
My mind is a space-ship now.
Just yesterday I was in the trees,
then I came down onto the plain.
I learned to throw things to get my food,
and I looked in awe
at the winking stars.
I lived out the arc of my little life.
I opened a future I could not see,
and could not imagine,
and could not conceive.
Now I perch on my chair in the fading night,
filled with wonder at the miracles
that shimmer, unfold
on this marvelous Earth,
all around that very same me.

48

Achievement is over-rated.
After you have exerted yourself
and triumphed and won the gold,
another day then follows.
A fresh, new scene is opened.
Your gaudy success recedes into
the dust-bin of history.
The world just keeps on unfolding.
Metamorphosis is the king.
True satisfaction comes in alignment
with the Presence of life unseen.
It's the only thing in the whole wide world
that continues, unfazed, forever.

49

We live our lives on a moving wave,
surfing as best we can.
We're carried by surging power
that propels us toward the land.
It's hard to keep our footing.
We are vulnerable every minute.
Absorbed on our board,
it is hard to see
that our destination and purpose in life
lies in Mystery, Mystery, Mystery.

50

The world is a shifting kaleidoscope.
The patterns change.
Our life unfolds.
We are moved from the depths
on our journey through time,
learning,
suffering,
hit with the unexpected
and the deeply painful.
Somehow we keep ourselves going,
though our resources may be strained.
We live it through
as best we can.
We live it a day at a time.
We are all on this journey together,
unfolding our precious life-span.

51

Why is it we feel that we must achieve
to acquire some status and worth?
We carry a hole
in the depths of our soul,
and it cries out for recognition.
But what if there is no hole?
What if we are, innately, complete?
What if our value is already there,
as children of the swirling suns,
and a Cosmos that has us in Its care?

52

Can writing poems make a difference?
How could that happen today?
The world does believe
that you only achieve
by working in materiality.
But there is more here
than meets the eye.
Reality is deeper than matter.
Our consciousness is changing,
and growing,
and expanding,
into new and unseen corridors.
Soon we will see
that what we will be
is here in potential now,
rising to Reality,
as unfolding, conscious dream.

53

The depth of Being is bottomless.
The sky reaches to infinity.
Our primate minds are learning
to look at the stars without fear.
The vastness has been over-whelming.
Its emptiness was a given.
But now we know
that it is not so.
Space is full of life, not empty.
It is teeming everywhere.
We are in a Sea
of Infinity,
alive, aware and unfolding.

54

Truth comes wrapped in Beauty.
The patterns beneath
the crust of the world
come forth with order and grace.
The elegance of the Unseen World
is always hoving into view,
coming with Its loveliness,
and harmony and splendor too.

55

Something is pouring out of me now.
Something is teaching me how
to reach my depths
and plumb my skies,
and reach into the heart of Mystery.
It's quite a state I'm in.
It's quite beyond my kin.
Something that is far greater than me
is pushing into the world to be,
and in the process of emerging forth
is teaching me
how to be free.

56

The surfaces of the world
shine and glitter,
singing a Siren's song
and demanding all our attention.
It's easy to see
why we foolishly think
that this is all of Reality's scope.
But Reality is a layered thing.
Its depths cannot be seen.
The Forces of Life lie simmering
in the levels below our sight.
The future is waiting invisibly there
to emerge into the light.

57

I want to create a beautiful thing.
The impulse is clearly not mine.
It moves through me
but I cannot see
its source, its origin.
I only know that I can feel
in my cells and nerves and mind
a pressing Force that is moving me
to bring this thing to be.
We're all in the grip
of a nameless Force
that is fueling our expression.

58

Don't come to Earth on a whim.
Think before you do it.
The experience here is rough
and tough,
not for the meek or mild.
Expect to be hit,
and tossed,
and burned,
as you make your way
through your every day.
You will feel fear,
and pain,
and loss,
but you will feel ecstasy too.
You really won't want to miss it.
It's truly worth a visit.

59

Tomorrow's world is here today,
enfolded in potential.
As we human beings make our way
into the unknown land,
we are fashioned by
an unseen Hand.
Our shapes are shifted.
Our minds expand.
We cannot see
what we will become.
We are caught in metamorphosis.
Raise your eyes
and expand your view.
Get beyond your little life.
You are caught in a process
that is mysterious,
and profound,
and powerful,
and lovely.
It is throwing up the world right now.
It is throwing up even you.

60

Change is frightening to us.
If we had our way
we'd prefer to have
every day
like every other.
Or would we?
Wouldn't life be suddenly
stultifying,
and stagnant,
and boring beyond belief?
If the prospect of change
was taken away,
our hopes and our dreams
would become passé.
No, I think that we would rather
be caught in the present, shifting game.
We would have to give up
much too much
if every day was just the same.

61

For the future to arrive
the present must be cracked,
and taken apart,
piece by precious piece,
disassembled to make a space
for the future to take its place.
But this scares us beyond belief.
Buddha saw deeply into things
when he said that change was king.
Incessant,
destructive,
eroding the now,
Life is moving us
always into the unknown.

62

What can we hang onto?
How can we keep our feet?
We're caught in a world,
a maelstrom of change,
that is constantly shifting the game.
Where can we find some safety?
Where is stability?
Perhaps we must look beyond the world
to the realm of invisibility.
The eternal Sea is around us,
beyond the shifting of time.
What could be safer, more stable,
than the arms of the Divine?
Raise your eyes and open your mind.
Look past the changing world.
There is nothing here but the Sea of Life,
basking in unchanging eternity.

63

Get with the flow.
Touch Living Being,
or figure out how to find It.
It won't be in the shoe stores,
or in the cocktail parties,
or in the coffee klatches.
You must find a way to go deeper.
It's better to do it alone.
The flow comes forth
from touching the Source.
Move yourself that way now.

64

How can I wake my mind?
I've been given this gift
of consciousness.
I should be in a state of bliss.
Why is it, then,
that I feel so bland,
so dull and dark,
so numb?
My mind is asleep to miracle.
My eyes are fixed on my toes.
I'm caught in a box of smallness.
And my discontent with it grows.
I must shake myself awake.
I must blow through my edges now.
I'm ready to wake up
and see the Truth
of Reality's magnificence.

65

The earth and I
are spinning through space.
You billions are spinning too.
We're whirling in a dance
of chance,
and trying to get a view
of the core of the world's Reality,
never mind that It's not material.
If we can't see It with our eyes,
we can feel it with our hearts.
The Real is here in this moment
It's all around us now.
We could just turn and see It,
But we can't figure out just how.

66

Mysterious me.
Mysterious we.
Mysterious world around us.
Something is spilling into our life
that fires our minds,
that beats our hearts,
that moves us through our days.
We are held here
by a Mystery
that we cannot see,
but must surely be
the Source of our humanity.

67

Who knew that it would be so hard?
Who knew that the ones
that we love best
would disappear over the hill?
Who knew that our
cherished hopes and dreams
would all come tumbling down?
Who knew that the things we yearn most for
were nowhere to be found?
We came,
we grew,
we hoped to have
a life that would be all Spring.
But reality is something different,
and harsher,
and less satisfying,
and more threatening
than we could have imagined.
Perhaps the problem
is with our expectations.

68

Somewhere galaxies are colliding
in seismic catastrophe.
Somewhere stars are bursting
and hurling themselves into night.
The Cosmos is building Itself right now
in violent, tumultuous ways.
This makes us a little uncomfortable.
We'd rather It be benign.
But the Force that is engaged
in throwing us up
has a cataclysmic, furious side.
It is stormy and ferocious.
It is all things that
we can see and imagine,
including the dark and destructive.
We can only watch in awe.

69

Like bubbles in liquid the impulses rise,
propelling me into motion.
I thought it was I
that was living my life,
but now I clearly see
that the driving Force
that is moving me
comes out of the Cosmic Sea.

70

Emptiness all around us.
It's enough to drive us crazy.
We are told every day
in every possible way
that we live in a void of deadness.
This is not a fit Cosmos to live in.
I refuse to play this game.
The context around us
is Life, Life, Life,
and the Cosmos is the same.

71

I want to see my consciousness.
I want to see what's in my head,
miraculous,
crucial,
invisible,
residing just under my hair.
I know that this Field is alive.
I know It is generative.
I know that my time here
depends on It.
It gives me my chance to live.
I think that this Field
is not just in me.
It's primary to the Cosmos.
It fills my head,
It fills the world,
and It fills the Cosmic Sea.

72

Have you ever watched a fire dance,
licking and jumping over the logs?
What's that all about?
It's not exactly space.
It's not exactly matter.
It's something between the two,
flaring and waving
flickering and burning,
and turning a log into warmth and light.
Radiance is appearing.
I'll bet you didn't realize
you were watching miracle.
The familiar in life
dulls our eyes and our minds
and leads us to take for granted
the marvels all around us,
the wondrous things of this earth.

73

I do not write the poem.
I open to receive it.
If I can empty myself
and make my mind clear,
and turn off my will
the poem will appear,
thrown up from the depths
of Living Space
above and below,
and from every place
all around me.

74

The culture is the World of Lies.
When we turn to it to ask:
"What should I do in my many days
with my one and precious life?"
The culture responds:
"Make money!
Buy things!
Get status!
Be famous!"
Not a word about wonder,
the shimmering Cosmos,
the miracle of our Life.
Not a word about basic Reality,
the infinite, living Cosmic Sea.

75

Can I ever be free
of the little me
who seems desperate
to be noticed?
My life should be deeper than that.
I am so vastly incomplete.
I still am caught by trivial things,
while I'm seaching for my value.
I should know better than that.
I should be bigger than that.
If I could,
and I would,
I could give up this game.
I've spent decades in its thrall.
I think at this age
I might finally see
the richness residing in Mystery.
I might finally open to Cosmic Life.
I might take myself beyond the small.

76

How do we know
when a phase is over
in our turbulent, unfolding life?
Something seems to be moving us
through the arc of our many days,
opening doors,
closing doors,
metamorphosing us
and re-making us
in a thousand myriad ways.
We are a moment in eternity,
fashioned now by Mystery.
Our life is what it will be
for reasons that we cannot see.

77

Let's raise our eyes from the mundane world.
Let's wake ourselves from our sleep.
We are evolving and metamorphosing.
We have appointments we must keep.
Before we step off the lovely earth
to become the swirling galaxies,
we must try to expand ourselves.
We must touch the Ocean of Livingness.
We must open to Its bliss.
We must throw ourselves in motion
to experience the mysterious Ocean.
It's for this we came.